RATH RUde
VICTORIAN
Limericks

Brian A. Lee - Blackmore

Published in the UK by
POWERFRESH Limited
Unit 3, Everdon Park,
Heartlands Industrial Estate,
Daventry
NN11 5YJ

Telephone   01327 871 777
Facsimile   01327 879 222
E Mail info@powerfresh.co.uk

ISBN   1904967256

Printed in Slovakia By Polygraf / Production service ZoneS
Powerfresh   July 2005

The truest observation about limericks was actually made in a limerick:

A limerick packs laughs anatomical
Into space that is quite economical.
But the good ones I've seen
So seldom are clean,
And the clean ones so seldom are comical.

Why perfect alliteration and hysterically funny punch lines are common factors in what are viewed by many as highly obscene and disgusting rhymes is often to do with the fact that the obscene Limerick is in reality the most widespread. The proliferation of this form of five line nonsense verse was the greater because Limericks easily lend themselves to composition by those who would ordinarily have little poetic ability. From bakers to bricklayers — everyone can do it. Likewise, they are an ideal platform for those with some talent, education and a broad vocabulary. Curates and Cardinals are as much culprits in this as their lesser brethren. As such, out of the millions of Limericks that have been composed since the end of the 19th century (and the Victorian and Edwardian Limerick predominates here), the larger number of brilliant, well-formed and superbly rhythmical examples are obscene. That so many persist, as a form of social communication, is testament to the fact that there is much humour and enjoyment to be found in them. This remains true irrespective of, and perhaps despite the fact that, they are undeniably obscene and sometimes relate to things that we find abhorrent, distasteful or unsettling. The fact is, this aspect is often softened by the shear brilliance of the compositional approach. In the best ones the crudity and obscenity become incidental, and we stand amazed and entertained by the 'laughs anatomical' in a 'space economical'.

Though coarseness and vulgarity win easily in terms of the social retention and longevity of such verse, it is not essential, and there are a number of equally admirable Limericks which are able to incorporate all the qualities of the best without resorting to anything crude or offensive. Of these, this collection includes a few of those better known. Recognized as witty and clever, these particular examples demonstrate that there is not a complete dearth of comparable cleverness.

It would be quite naive to assume that these five line verses were originated wholly by Edward Lear in his Book of Nonsense in 1846 although the word Limerick might well be a corruption of "Learick". However, there appear to be earlier historical precedents, there being some evidence that the form was known as early as the 1690's. At that time, soldiers of the "Irish Brigade", who were recruited in the town of Limerick and sent to France, eventually brought back a type of five line verse already popular at the time and similar to a French verse form and the English nursery rhyme. Indeed, the English nursery rhyme, such as *Hickory, Dickory, Dock* - etc, is a close relative as a five line rhyme but antedates any limerick *per se* by hundreds of years. As the years passed, the five line verse took on a persuasive popularity whether obscene or not. Party games and national competitions in the late 19th and early part of the 20th centuries extemporizing on a pre-set pair of lines, have also been a rich and fertile source of limericks. Strange it is, that the most durable appear to be those which are risqué, and the best of those the ones which take us to the edge of tolerance and acceptance and yet redeem themselves as admirable pieces of humour or poetry.

As a note to the reader, these examples herein are as found or learnt by the author, either through word of mouth or in the numerous British and US anthologies and collections that have appeared in the past. Not only is this selection a perspective on the variety of forms to be found, it confirms that there are likely to be many versions of one particular Limerick in circulation. This can be confusing since, too often, lines of one may be borrowed from another or the pattern of rhyme or alliteration is similar.

Where possible in this collection, the original has been used though it remains true that later, or alternative, versions may be more polished and elegant. Finally, there are many, many examples that have been excluded because they rely too much on profanities, obscenities and blasphemy or reflect too much a disturbed mind. The criteria we set are simple, is it funny, is it clever, does it show merit above its vulgarity? If so, you will find it here!

Brian. A. Lee-Blackmore 2004

There was a young man from Poole,
Who found a Red Ring on his Tool,
The Doctor, a Cynic,
Said "Get out of my Clinic,
And Wipe off the Lipstick you Fool!"

I went to the Duchess for tea,
She said "Do you fart when you pee?"
I said "Not a bit,
Do you grunt when you shit?"
And felt it was one up for me.

A mortician who practised in Fife
Made love to the corpse of his wife.
"I couldn't know Judge!
She just didn't budge!"
It was just as she'd acted in life."

Two young rakes from Upingham
Stood on the bridge at Buckingham
Watching the stunts
Of the cunts in the punts
And the tricks of the pricks that were fucking 'em

A weird schizophrenic said, "Me?
I am not that I am, I'm a tree."
But another, more sane,
Exclaimed , "I'm a Great Dane"
And covered his leg with wee.

Said the venerable Dean of Saint Paul's,
"Concerning the cracks in the walls -,
Do you think it would do,
If we filled them with glue?"
The Bishop of Lincoln said "Balls!"

A beautiful belle of Del Norte
Is reckoned disdainful and haughty
Because during the day,
She says: "Boys, keep away!"
But she fucks in the gloaming — quite naughty!

A beautiful lady named Psyche
Is loved by a fellow named Ikey.
One thing about Ike
The lady can't like
Is his prick, which is dreadfully spikey.

A big-bosomed Bunny named Gression
Sold cigars at a key-club con-cession.
When she swiveled about
Even strong men cried out,
For her costume could not keep her flesh in.

A bobby of Nottingham Junction
Whose organ had long ceased to function
Deceived his good wife
For the rest of her life
With the aid of his constable's truncheon.

A broken-down harlot named Tupps
Was heard to confess in her cups:
"The height of my folly
Was diddling a collie-
Now what price do I ask for the pups?"

A busy young lady named Gloria
Was had by Sir Gerald du Maurier
And then by six men,
Sir Gerald again,
And the band at the Waldorf-Astoria.

A cabin boy aboard an old Clipper
Grew steadily more flipper and flipper.
He plugged up his ass
With fragments of glass
And thus circumcised his randy old skipper.

A cautious young fellow named Leep
Had seatbelts installed in his Jeep.
When his date was strapped in,
He committed a sin,
With the gear stick and part of his seat.

A cautious young fellow named Tunney
Had a whang that was worth any money.
When eased in half-way,
The girl's sigh had him say,
"Why the sigh?" "For the rest of it, honey."

A certain young person of Ghent,
Uncertain if lady or gent,
Shows his organs at large
For a small handling charge
To assist him in paying the rent.

A certain young Sheik of Algiers
Said to his harem, "Listen my dears,
Though it may well be odd of me,
I'm tired of just sodomy
Let's try straight fucking." (loud cheers!)

Then up spoke the Bay of Algiers,
"I am old and well stricken in years,
And my language is blunt
But a cunt is a cunt,
And fucking is fucking" (loud cheers).

A chap down in old Oklahoma
Had a cock that could sing 'La Paloma',
But the sweetness of pitch
Couldn't put off the hitch
Of impotence, size and aroma.

A charmer from old Amarillo,
Sick of finding strange heads on her pillow,
Decided one day
That to keep men away
She would stuff up her crevice with Brillo.

A waitress who worked in North Bluff
Had a pussy as large as a muff.
It had room for both hands
And some intimate glands,
And was soft as a little duck's fluff.

A clever young man named Eugene
Invented a wanking machine.
On the twenty-third stroke
The fuckin' thing broke
And beat both his balls to a cream.

A cocksucking steno' named Beeman
Remarked as she swallowed my semen :
"On my minuscule salary
I must watch every calorie,
So I get `ahead' eating you he-men!"

A contortionist hailing from Lynch
Used to rent out his tool by the inch.
A foot cost a quid —
He could and he did
Often stretch it to three (at a pinch!).

A couple was fishing near Clombe
When the maid began looking quite glum,
And said, "Bother the fish!
I'd rather coish!"
Which they did — which was why they had come.

A cowhand way out in Seattle
Had a dick as flat as a paddle.
Said he" I can't fuck -
A lamb or a duck,
But golly, it just fits the cattle!"

A Crusader's wife out from the garrison
Had an affair with a hairy old Saracen.
She was not oversexed,
Or jealous or vexed,
She just wanted to make a comparison.

A miniscule man from Samora
Had a cock of one inch and no morea.
It was good for keyholes
And debutantes' peeholes
But not worth a damn as a borer.

A daredevil skater named Lowe,
Leaps barrels arranged in the snow,
But is proudest of doing,
Some incredible screwing,
Since he's jumped thirteen girls in a row!

A deep-throated virgin named Netty
Was sucking a cock on the jetty.
She said, "It tastes nice,
Much better than rice,
Though not quite so good as spaghetti."

A delighted, incredulous bride
Remarked to her groom "I've espied —" :
Though I never could quite
Believe till tonight
That your   outsized my inside."

A Dentist — young Doctor Malone,
Got a charming girl patient alone,
And, in his depravity,
Filled the wrong cavity.
God, how his practice has grown!

A despairing old landlord named Fyffe,
With a frigid and quarrelsome wife,
Let his third-story front,
To a willing young cunt,
Who supplied him a new lease on life!

A desperate spinster from Clare
Once knelt in the moonlight all bare,
And prayed to her God
For a romp on the sod —
T'was a passerby answered her prayer.

A distinguished professor from Swarthmore
Got along with a sexy young sophomore.
As quick as a glance
He stripped off his pants,
But found that the sophomore'd already got off
more.

A doctoral student from Buckingham
Wrote his thesis on cunts and on fucking 'em.
But a dropout from Paree
Taught him Gamahuchee
So he added a footnote on sucking 'em.

A do-it-yourselfer named Alice,
Used a dynamite stick for a phallus.
She blew her vagina
To South Carolina,
And her tits landed somewhere in Dallas.

There once was a girl from Spitzbergen,
Whom people all thought a Virgin
Till they found her in bed,
With her quim very red,
And the head of a child emergin',

There once was a girl from Kilkenny,
Whose usual charge was one penny,
For half of that sum,
You might roger her bum,
A source of amusement to many!

A cute friend of hers, Fanny Hill,
Used two dynamite sticks for a dil.
They found her vagina,
In South Carolina,
And part of her ass in Brazil.

A dolly in Dallas named Alice,
Whose overworked sex is all callous,
Wore the foreskin away
On uncircumcised Ray,
Through exuberance, tightness, and malice.

A dulcet-voiced call-girl named Shedd,
Who's cultured, well-spoken, well-bred,
Had achieved some renown
For her tone, going down—
There's a nice civil tongue in her head.

A fair-haired young damsel named Grace
Thought it very, very foolish to place
Her hand on your cock
When it turned hard as rock,
For fear it would explode in your face.

A farmer I know named O'Doul
Had a long and incredible tool.
He can use it to plow,
Or to diddle a cow,
Or just as a cue-stick at pool.

A fellatrix's healthful condition
Proved the value of spunk as nutrition.
Her remarkable diet
(I suggest that you try it)
Was solely her clients' emission.

A fellow whose surname was Hunt
Trained his cock to perform a slick stunt:
This versatile spout
Could be turned inside out,
Like a glove, and be used as a punt.

A fisherman off of Cape Cod
Said, "I'll bugger that tuna, by God!"
But the high-minded fish
Resented his wish,
And nimbly swam off with his rod.

A foolish geologist from Kissen
Just didn't know what he was missin',
By studying rock
And neglecting his cock,
And using it merely for pissin'.

There was an old man of the Cape,
Who buggered a Barbary Ape,
Said the Ape "Sir, your prick,
Is too long and too thick,
And something is wrong with the shape!"

There was an old man of the Cape,
Who buggered a Barbary Ape,
The Ape said "You fool,
You've got a square tool,
You've buggered my arse out of shape!"

A bad little girl in Madrid,
A most reprehensible kid,
Told her Tante Louise
That her clit smelled like cheese,
And the worst of it was, that it did!

A gay young prince from Morocco
Made love in a manner rococo.
He painted his penis
To resemble a venus
And flavored his semen with cocoa.

A geneticist living in Delft
Scientifically played with himself,
And when he was done
He labeled it: son,
And filed it away on a shelf.

A German composer named Bruckner
Remarked to a lady while fucking her :
"Less lento, my dear,
With your cute little rear;
I like a hot presto — may I suck on her?"

A gifted young fellow from Sparta
Was widely renowned as a farta'.
He could fart anything
From "Of Thee Do I Sing,"
To Beethoven's "Moonlight Sonata."

A graduate student named Zac
Was said to be great in the sack.
An inch of his boner
Put girls in a coma
Just two gave them orgasmic attacks.

A greedy young lady from Sidney
Liked it in — right up to her kidney,
Till a man from Quebec
Shoved it up to her neck—
He really diddled her, didn' he?

A green-thumbed young farmer from Leeds
Once swallowed a packet of seeds.
In a month, his large arse
Was covered with grass
And his balls were grown over with weeds.

A habit depraved and unsavory
Held the bishop of Bingham in slavery
Midst screeches and howls
He deflowered young owls
Which he kept in an underground aviary

A habit obscene and bizarre,
Has taken a-hold of papa.
He brings home young camels
And other odd mammals,
And gives them a go at mama.

A happy old hooker named Grace
Once sponsored a cunt-lapping race.
It was hard for beginners
To tell who were winners :
There were cunt hairs all over the place.

A haughty young wench of Del Norte
Would only fuck men over forty.
Said she, "It's too quick
With a young fellow's prick;
I like it to last, and be warty."

A hearty paranormal named Most
Had an affair with a nice nympho ghost.
At the height of the spasm
The poor ectoplasm
Cried, "Goodie, I feel it ... almost."

Then up spake the King of Spain,
"To fuck and to bugger is pain,
But it's not infra-dig,
On occasion to frig,
And to do it again and again."

A hidebound young virgin named Carrie
Would say, when the fellows got hairy :
"Keep your prick in your pants
Till the end of this dance—"
Which is why Carrie still has her sweet cherry.

A highly aesthetic young Jew
Had eyes of heavenly blue;
The end of his dillie
Was shaped like a lilly,
And his balls looked like flowers too!

A horny young fellow named Reg,
Was jerking off under a hedge.
The gardener drew near
With a huge pruning shear,
And trimmed off the edge of his wedge.

A large organed female from Dallas,
Named Alice, who yearned for a phallus,
Was virgo intacto,
Because, ipso facto,
No phallus in Dallas fits Alice.

A lacklustre lady of Brougham
Labours all night at her loom.
Anon she doth blanch
When her lord and his wench
Pull a chain in the neighbouring room.

A lad, at his first copulation,
Cried, "Golly what a sensation!,
It's gyration - elation,
Throughout the duration,
I guess I'll give up masturbation."

A lad from far-off Transvaal
Was lustful, but tactful withal.
He'd say, just for luck,
"Mam'selle, do you fuck?"
But too often got a kick in the ball.

A lad of the brainier kind
Had erogenous zones on his mind.
He got his sensations,
By solving equations,
(Of course, in the end, he went blind.)

A lady from old Kalamazoo
Found she had little or nothing to do,
So she sat on the stairs
And counted her hairs:
4,302.

A lady from Newmantle Rock
Of fidelity took very little stock,
She deserted her man
In the streets of Japan
For a boy with a prehensile cock.

A stockholder lady sex-hetera
Decided her fortune to bettera:
On the floor, quite unclad,
She successively had
Merrill Lynch, Pierce, Fenner, et cetera...

A lady while dining at Crewe
Found an elephant's dick in her stew.
Said the waiter, "Don't shout,
And don't wave it about,
Or the others will all want one too."

A lady with features cherubic
Was famed for her area pubic.
When they asked her its size
She replied in surprise,
"Are you speaking of square feet, or cubic?"

A lass at the foot of her class
Asked a brainier chick how to pass.
She replied, "With no fuss
You can get a B-plus,
By letting the Prof. pat your ass."

A lecherous barkeep named Dale,
After fucking his favorite female,
Mixed Drambuie and scotch
With the cream in her crotch
For a lustier, Rusty-er Nail.

A licentious old justice of Salem
Used to catch all the harlots and jail 'em.
But instead of a fine
He would stand them in line,
With his common-law tool to impale 'em.

A lonely young lad of Eton
Used always to sleep with the heat on,
Till he ran into a lass
Who showed him her ass —
Now they sleep with only a sheet on.

A lovely young diver named Nancy,
Wore a bikini bottom quite chancy,
The fish of Bonaire,
Watched her Derriere,
And the sea fans all tickled her fancy.

A lusty young maid from Seattle
Got pleasure by sleeping with cattle;
Till she found a big bull
Who filled her so full
It made both her ovaries rattle.

A lusty young woodsman named Staine
For years with no woman had lain,
But he found sublimation
At a high elevation
At the top of a Pine — God, the pain!

A madam who ran a bordello
Put cum in her pineapple jellos,
For the rich, sexy taste
And not wanting to waste
The gallons of cream from her fellows .

A maestro directing in Rome
Had a quaint way of driving it home.
Whoever he climbed
Had to keep her tail timed
To the beat of his old metronome.

A maiden who lived in Virginny
Had a cunt that could bark, neigh and whinny.
The horse lovers rushed her,
But success finally crushed her
For her tone soon became harsh and tinny.

A maiden who traveled in France
Once got on a train, just by chance.
The engineer fucked her,
The conductor sucked her,
And the fireman came off in his pants.

A maiden who wrote of big cities
Sang songs full of love, fun and pities,
Sold her stuff at the shop
Of a musical wop
Who played with her soft little titties.

A marine being sent to Hong Kong
Got a doctor to alter his dong.
He sailed off with a tool
Flat and thin as a rule -
When he got there he found he was wrong.

A young mathematician named Hall
Had a dodecahedral ball,
The weight of his pecker.
Plus his balls altogether,
Was four-fifths of nine-tenths of fuck-all!

An odd mathematician named Klein
Thought the Mobius Strip too divine.
Said he, "If you glue
The edges of two,
You'll get a weird shaped bottle like mine!

A middle-aged codger named Bruin
Found his love life completely in ruin,
For he flirted with flirts
Wearing pants and no skirts,
And he never went in for screwin'.

There once was a lady of Ealing,
Who had a peculiar feeling,
She lay on her back,
And opened her crack
And pissed from the floor to the ceiling.

There was a young man of Loch Leven,
Who went for a walk — about seven,
He fell into a pit,
That was brimful of shit,
Now the poor buggers walking in heaven

A milkmaid there was, with a stutter,
Who was lonely and wanted a flutter.
She had nowhere to turn,
So she diddled a churn,
And managed to come with the butter.

A nasty old drunk in Carmel
Thinks it funny to piss in the well.
He says, "Some don't favour
The unusual flavour,
But I don't drink the stuff — what the hell!"

A nervous young fellow named Fred
Took a charming young widow to bed.
When he'd diddled a while
She remarked with a smile,
"You've got it all in but the head."

A newlywed couple from Goshen
Spent their honeymoon sailing the ocean.
In twenty-eight days
They got laid eighty ways —
Imagine such fucking devotion!

A newly-wed man of Peru
Found himself in a terrible stew:
His wife was in bed
Much deader than dead,
And so he had no one to screw.

A notorious whore named Ms. Hearst,
In the pleasures of men was well-versed.
Reads the sign o'er the head
Of her well-rumpled bed
"The customer always comes first."

A sex-hungry novice saw the Abbot:
"Now, consider the goat and the rabbit.
While they roll in the hay
You stay home and pray.
You've got to get out of that habit!"

A nudist resort at Benares
Took a midget in all unawares.
But he made members weep
For he just couldn't keep
His nose out of their private affairs.

A pansy who lived in Khartoum
Took a lesbian up to his room.
They argued all night
Over who had the right
To do what, with which, and to whom.

A passionate young red-headed girl
When you kissed her, her senses would whirl,
And her twat would get wet,
And would wiggle and fret,
And her cunt-lips would curl and unfurl.

A pathetic old maid of Bordeaux
Fell in love with a dashing young beau.
To arrest his regard
She would squat in his yard
And longingly pee in the snow.

A petulant man said, "I feign,
Your cunt is the size of a lane."
She replied, "Why, you fool,
With your meagre little tool,
It's like pushing a pin down a drain.."

A physical fellow named Fisk
Could screw at a rate very brisk.
So fast was his action
The Fitzgerald contraction
Would shrink up his rod to a disc.

A pious old woman named Tweak
Had taught her vagina to speak.
It was frequently liable
To quote from the Bible,
But when fucking — not even a squeak!

A pious young lady named Finnegan
Would caution her friend, "Well, you're in again;
So time it aright,
Make it last through the night,
For I certainly don't want to sin again!"

A pious young lady of Chichester
Made all of the saints in their niches stir
And each morning at matin
Her breast in pink satin
Made the clergy and bishop's breeches stir.

A plumber whose name was John Brink
Plumbed the cook as she bent o'er the sink.
Her resistance was stout,
And John Brink petered out,
With his pipe-wrench all limber and pink.

A potter who lived in Bombay
Fashioned a vagina out of straw and wet clay;
But the heat of his dick
Kilned the damn thing to brick
And chafed all his foreskin away.

A pretty wife living in Tours
Demanded her daily amour.
But the husband said, "No!
It's to much, let go!
My balls are hitting the floor."

A pretty young lady named Vogel
Once sat herself down on a molehill.
A curious mole
Nosed into her hole —
Ms. Vogel's okay, but the mole's ill.

A pretty young maiden from France
Decided she'd "just take a chance."
She let herself go
For an hour or so,
And now all her sisters are aunts.

A princess who reigned in Baroda
Made her home on a purple pagoda.
She festooned the walls
Of her halls, with the balls,
Of the tools of the fools who bestrode her.

A progressive professor named Winners
Held classes each evening for sinners.
They were graded and spaced
So the vile and debased
Would not be held back by beginners.

A rapist who reeked of cheap booze
Attempted to ravish Miss Hughes.
She cried, "I suppose
There's no time for my clothes,
But PLEASE let me take off my shoes!"

A rapturous and determined young fellatrix
Was one day at work on five pricks.
With an unholy cry
She whipped out her glass eye:
"Tell the boys I can now take on six."

There was a young girl who would make,
Advances to snake after snake,
She said "I'm not really vicious,
But _so_ superstitious,
I just do it for grandmothers sake!"

A reckless young lady of Mance,
Had no qualms about taking a chance,
But she thought it was crude
To get screwed in the nude,
So she always went home with damp pants.

A remarkable race are the Persians;
They have such peculiar diversions.
They make love all the day
In the usual way
And save up the nights for perversions.

A responsive young girl from the East
In bed was an able artiste.
She had learned two positions
From family physicians,
And ten more from the old parish priest.

A romantic attraction has clung
To a chap of whom damsels have sung:
"'Tis the Scourge from the East,
That lascivious beast
Who was known as Attila the Hung!"

A sailor who slept in the sun,
Woke to find his fly buttons undone,
He remarked with a smile,
"Good grief, a sun-dial!
And now it's a quarter-past one."

A savvy young hooker named Gail
Got busted and lodged in the jail.
But the jailer got hot,
To be lodged in her twat,
And so Gail made the bail with her tail.

A scandal involving an oyster
Sent the Countess of Clews to a cloister
She preferred it, in bed,
To the count (so she said)
'Cause it's longer and stronger and moister.

A scream from the crypt of St. Giles
Resounded for miles upon miles.
Said the friar, "Good gracious,
The brother Ignatius
Forgeteth the abbot hath piles."

A silly young man from Hong Kong
Had hands that were skinny and long.
He ate rice with his fingers—
The taste of it lingers,
But now all his fingers are gone.

A space shuttle pilot named Ventry,
Made love to a lovely girl sentry.
She started to pout,
Because it fell out,
But the mission was saved by re-entry.

A sperm faced (alack and forsooth),
His moment of sexual truth.
He'd expected to fall
On a womb's spongy wall
But was dashed to his death on a tooth.

A spinster in old Kalamazoo
Once strolled after dark by the zoo.
She was seized by the nape,
And fucked by an ape,
And she murmured, "A wonderful screw."

A spunky young schoolboy named Fred
Used to toss off each night while in bed.
Said his mother, "Dear lad,
That's exceedingly bad—
Jump in here with your mamma instead."

A starship commander named Kirk
Emerged from his cabin berserk.
He grabbed a girl yeoman
Beneath the abdomen,
And gave her a physical jerk.

A studious professor named Nestor
Bet a whore all his books that he could best her.
But she drained out his balls
And skipped up the walls,
Beseeching poor Nestor to rest her.

A sweety named Countess de Marden,
Went down on her lover in the garden.
He said, "Good lord, Tess,
Please don't swallow that mess "
She replied, "Ulp - I beg your pardon?"

A talented fuckstress, Miss Chisholm,
Was renowned for her fine paroxysm.
While the man laid at rest,
She went on with some zest,
Till she came and his dick formed a schism

A talented girl from Detroit
Could fuck you in ways quite adroit.
She could squeeze her vagina
To a pin-point or finer
Or open it out like a quoit.

A thrice-married gal from L.A.
Said, "My hymen's intact for the day,
'Cause my first simply talked of it,
The voyeur just gawked at it,
And my most recent man's a gourmet."

A tired young trollop of Nome
Was worn out from her toes to her dome.
Eight miners came screwing,
But she said, "Nothing doing;
Sorry - one of you will have to go home!"

A half-cast trapper named Feber,
Once captured and buggered a Beaver.
The result of this fuck
Was a three titted duck,
A canoe, and an Irish Retriever.

A very odd pair are the Pitts:
His balls are as large as her tits,
Her tits are as large
As a forty foot barge—
Neither knows how the other one fits.

A wanton young lady from Wimley
Reproached for not acting quite primly
Said, "Heavens above!
I know sex isn't love,
But it's such an entrancing facsimile."

A weary old lecher named Blott
Took a luscious young blond to his yacht.
Too lazy to rape her,
He made darts out of paper,
Which he leisurely tossed at her twat.

A whimsical fellow named Bloch
Could beat the base drum with his cock.
With a special erection
He could play a selection
From Johann Sebastian Bach.

A wicked stone cutter named Cary
Drilled holes in divine statuary.
With eyes full of malice
He pulled out his phallus,
And buggered a stone Virgin Mary.

A wide-bottomed girl named Trasket
Had a hole as big as a basket.
A spot, as a bride,
In it now, you could hide,
And include with your luggage your mascot.

A wonderful tribe are the Sweenies,
Renowned for the length of their peenies.
The hair on their balls
Sweeps the floors of their halls,
But they don't look at women, the meanies.

A worn-out young husband named Lair
Heard daily his wife's plaintive prayer:
"Slip on a sheath, quick,
Then slip your big dick
Between these lips all covered in hair."

A young bride and groom of Australia
Remarked as they joined genitalia :
"Though the system seems odd,
We are thankful that God
Developed the genus Mammalia."

There once was a man of Cape-Horn,
Who wished he had never been born,
And he would not have been,
If his father had seen,
That the end of the rubber was worn.

A young lady sat by the sea,
Just as proper as proper could be.
A young fellow goosed her,
And roughly seduced her,
So she thanked him and went home to tea.

A young maiden from France was no prude,
She decided to dive in the nude,
But her buddy, behind,
Went out of his mind,
When he noticed where she was tattooed.

A young man by a girl was desired
To give her the thrills she required,
But he died of old age
Ere his cock could assuage
The volcanic desire it inspired.

A young man from the banks of the Po
Found his cock had elongated so,
That having a pee
It was never never he
But only his neighbors who'd know.

A young man maintained that his trigger
Was so big that there weren't any bigger.
But this poor flaccid dick
Was so heavy and thick
It hung down - in short, it lacked vigour.

A young man with passions quite gingery
Tore a hole in his sister's best lingerie.
He slapped her behind
And made up his mind
To add incest to insult and injury.

A young polo-player named Irkley
Made love to his sweetheart (beserkly).
In the midst of each chukker
He would break off and fuck her
Horizontally, laterally (and verkeley).

A young violinist from Rio
Was seducing a woman named Cleo.
As she took down her panties
She said, "No andantes;
I want this allegro con brio!"

A young wife in the outskirts of Arase
Preferred frigging to going to mass.
Said her husband, "Take Jock,
Or any young cock,
For I cannot live up to your ass."

A young woman got married at Chester,
Her mother she kissed her and blessed her.
Says she, "You're in luck,
He's a stunning good fuck,
For I had him myself down in Leicester."

Alas for the Countess d'Isere,
Whose muff wasn't furnished with hair.
Said the Count, "Quelle surprise!"
When he parted her thighs;
"Magnifique! Pourtant pas de la guerre."

All the female apes ran from King Kong
For his dong was unspeakably long.
But a friendly giraffe
Quaffed his yard and a half,
And ecstatically burst into song.

There once was a man of Toledo,
Who was cursed with an excessive libido,
To fuck and to screw,
And to fornicate too,
Were the three major planks of his credo.

An agreeable girl named Miss Doves
Likes to jack off the young men she loves.
She will use her bare fist
If the fellows insist
But she really prefers to wear gloves.

I am the Bishop of Ardleigh,
And though you mightn't think it of me,
I've a face like a lamb,
A cock like a ram
And a mind like a W.C.

An anaemic young lady of Stoke,
Who in favour of Chastity spoke,
By her Doctor was told.
"If I may be so bold,
What you need is a jolly good poke!"

A giant of a woman named Dunne
Let a midget screw her for fun.
But the poor little runt
Was engulfed in her cunt
And re-born as the twin of his son.

An ambitious lady named Harriet
Once dreamed she was raped in a chariot
By seventeen sailors
A monk and three tailors,
Mohammed and Judas Iscariot.

An architect fellow named Yoric
Could, when feeling euphoric,
Display for selection
Three kinds of erection-
Corinthian, Ionic, and Doric.

There is an old man of Uttoxeter,
Who curses his wife and throws socks at her,
When she dares to complain,
He adds to the pain,
By waving his balls and his cock at her.

An ardent young man named Magruder
Once wooed a girl nude in Bermuda.
She thought it quite lewd
To be wooed in the nude,
But magruder was shrewder, he screwed her.

There once was a man of Montrose,
Who could diddle himself with his toes,
He did it so neat,
He fell in love with his feet,
And christened them Myrtle and Rose.

An arrogant wench from Salt Lake
Liked to tease all the boys on the make.
She was finally the prize
Of a man twice her size
And all she recalls is the ache.

An artist who lived in Australia
Once painted his ass like a Dahlia.
The drawing was fine,
The colour - divine,
The scent - ah, but that was a failia.

Said the Reverend Jabez McCotten,
"Sex of the Devil begotten."
Said Jones to Miss Bly,
"Never mind the old guy;
To the pure almost everything's rotten."

There once was a son-of-a-bitch
Neither handsome nor clever nor rich,
Yet the Girls he would dazzle,
And fuck to a frazzle,
Then ditch them, the son-of-a-bitch!

An envious girl named McMeanus
Was jealous of her lover's big penis.
It was no consolation
That the rest of the nation
Of women were like her in weeness.

There once was a lady of Harwich,
Who said on the eve of her marriage,
"I shall sow my chemise,
Right down to my knees,
For I'm damned if I'll fuck in the carriage!"

There was an old lady of Bermuda,
Who shot a marauding intruder,
It was not through her ire,
At his lack of attire,
But his grabbing her jewels as he screwed her.

An impish young fellow named James
Had a passion for idiot games.
He lighted the hair
Of his lady's coiffeur
And laughed as she pissed through the flames.

When the Bermondsey bricklayer struck,
Bill Bloggins was 'avin' a fuck;
By union rules,
e'ad to lay down his tools —
Now wasn't that 'ard bleeding luck?

An impotent Scot named MacDougall
Had to husband his sperm and be frugal.
He was gathering semen
To gender a he-man,
By screwing his wife through a bugle.

An ingenious young man in South Bend
Made a synthetic ass for a friend,
But the friend shortly found
Its construction unsound,
It was simply a bother — no end.

An innocent maiden named Harridge
Was cruelly tricked into marriage;
When she later found out
What her spouse was about,
She threw herself under a carriage.

An inquisitive virgin named Dora
Asked the man who started to bore 'er :
"Do you mean birds and bees
Go through antics like these,
To supply us our fauna and flora?"

An irate young lady named Booker
Told her husband, "You beast, I'm no hooker!
If you want it queer ways,
Go to whores for your lays!"
So he packed up his tool and forsook 'er.

An old couple just at Shrovetide
We're having a shag — when he died.
The wife for a week
Sat tight on his peak,
And bounced up and down as she cried.

A bold and lecherous designer
Had thoughts on a minor named Dinah.
He couldn't carry them out
For his prick was too stout,
And too small was the minor's vagina.

An old maid who had a pet ape
Lived in fear of perpetual rape.
His red, hairy phallus
So filled her with malice
That she sealed up her snatch with Scotch tape.

An organist playing in York
Had a prick that could hold a small fork,
And between obbligatos
He'd munch at tomatoes,
To keep up his strength while at work.

An orgasmic young sex star named Sue
Was a hit as she writhed to a screw.
Her climatic fame spread
With an ad blitz that said:
Cuming soon at a theater near you!

There was a young lady named Sue,
Who preferred a stiff drink to a screw,
But one leads to another,
And now she's a mother,
Let that be a lesson to you!

An uptight young lady named Breerley
Who valued her morals too dearly
Had sex, so I hear,
Only once every year,
And it strained her vagina severely.

And earnest young woman in Thrace
Said, "Darling, that's not the right place!"
So he gave her a thwack,
And did on her back,
What he couldn't have done face to face.

And then there's the story that's fraught,
A tale of soft balls that got caught,
When a chap took a crap
In the woods, and a trap
Underneath... Oh, I can't bear the thought!

The pontiff with a priest from Norain,
Was queried "Is a sin so much a shame?"
If I screw a young nun
In the Eastertide sun?"
His holiness murmured, "Her name?."

At a contest for farting in Butte
One lady's exertion was cute :
It won the diploma
For fetid aroma,
And three judges were felled by the brute.

At a dance, a girl from New Circete
Showed an absolute absence of etiquette
Letting all comers press
Through the skirt of her dress
And wiping the mess with her petticoat.

At the moment Japan declared war
A sailor was fucking a whore.
He said, "After this poke
'Long and hard' ain't no joke;
This means months 'til I get back ashore."

Back in the days of old Adam
The grass served as mattress for madam,
And they spent the whole day
On the sex that today
Would bounce on box springs, if they had 'em.

Each Friday his engines abort,
But Scotty is never caught short.
He fills his machines
With space-navy beans,
And farts the ship back into port.

"Fucked by the finger of Fate!"
Bewailed a young fellow named Tate.
"Since dating Miss Baugh,
My whole tongue has been raw—
It must have been something I ate."

In the case of a lady named Frost,
Whose cunt's a good two feet acrost,
It's the best part of valor
To bugger the gal, or
You're apt to fall in and get lost.

In the Garden of Eden lay Adam,
Complacently stroking his madam,
And loud was his mirth
For on all of the earth
There were only two balls — and he had 'em.

It always delights me at Hank's
To walk up the old river banks.
One time in the grass
I stepped on an ass,
And heard a young girl murmur, "Thanks."

It had snowed, so the man in the drift,
Flagged her down and said, "Give me a lift?"
They sat in her Bentley,
She fondled him gently,
And the lift that he'd asked for was swift!

The late Brigham Young was no neuter —
No faggot, no fairy, no fruiter.
Where ten thousand virgins
Succumbed to his urgin's
There now stands the great State of Utah.

The latest reports from Good Hope
State their apes have pricks thick as a rope,
They fuck high and free,
From the top of one tree
To the top of the next — what a scope!

The old archeologist, Throstle,
Discovered a marvelous fossil.
He knew from its bend
And the knot on the end,
T'was the penis of Paul the Apostle.

There once was a bishop from Birmingham
Who deflowered young girls while confirming 'em.
As they knelt on the hassock
He lifted his cassock
And slipped his Episcopal worm in 'em.

There once was a boy named Carruther
Who was busily fucking his mother
"I know it's a sin,"
He said, shoving it in,
"But it's better than blowing my brother."

There once was a chick named Sillay,,
Who went out to Aspen to play.
Along came a Spyder,
Who sat down beside her
And she blew the poor bastard away.

There once was a clergyman's daughter
Who detested the pony he bought her,
Till she found that its dong
Was as hard and as long
As the prayers her father had taught her.

She married a fellow named Tony
Who soon found her fucking the pony.
Said he, "What's it got,
My dear, that I've not?"
Sighed she, "A yard more and it's quite bony!"

There once was a couple named Kelley,
Who lived their life belly to belly.
Because in their haste
They used library paste,
Instead of petroleum jelly.

There once was a lady of Brussels,
Who was proud of her vaginal muscles,
She could easily plex them,
And so interflex them,
And whistle love songs through her bustles.

There was a young fellow named Hort,
Had a dick although thick was quite short,
But to make up the loss,
He had balls like a hoss,
And he never shot less than a quart.

There once was a Duchess of Beever
Who slept with her golden retriever.
Said the potted old Duke :
"Such tricks make me puke!
Were it not for her money, I'd leave her."

There once was a Duchess of Bruges
Whose cunt was incredibly huge.
Said the king to this dame
As he thunderously came:
"Mon Dieu! Apres moi, le deluge!"

There once was a fairy named Avers
Who encircled his cock with lifesavers.
Though buggers all claimed
That their asses were maimed,
Sixy-niners all cheered the new flavours.

There once was a fellow named Bob
Who in sexual ways was a snob.
One day he was swimmin'
With twelve naked women
And deserted them all for a gob.

There once was a fellow named Brewster
Who said to his wife, as he goosed her,
"It used to be grand
But look at my hand
You're not wiping as clean as ya uster."

There once was a fellow named Howard,
Whose tool it was nuclear-powered,
While grabbing some ass,
He reached critical mass,
But think of the girl he deflowered!

There once was a fellow named Potts
Who was prone to having the trots
But his humble abode
Was without a commode
So his carpet was covered with spots.

There once was a fellow named Siegel
Who attempted to bugger a beagle,
But the mettlesome bitch
Turned and said with a twitch,
"It's fun, but you know it's illegal."

There once was a fellow named Sweeney
Who spilled gin all over his weenie.
Not being uncouth,
He added vermouth
And slipped his amour a martini.

There once was a fencer named Fisk,
Whose speed was incredibly brisk.
So fast was his action,
The Fitzgerald contraction,
Foreshortened his foil to a disk.

There once was a feisty young terrier
Who liked to bite girls on the derriere.
He'd yip and he'd yap,
Then leap up and snap;
And the fairer the derriere the merrier.

There once was a floozie named Annie
Whose prices were cozy—but cannie:
A buck for a fuck,
Fifty cents for a suck,
And a dime for a feel of her fanny.

There once was a freshman named Lin,
Whose tool was as thin as a pin,
A virgin named Joan
From a bible belt home,
Said "This won't be much of a sin."

There once was a gangster named Brown
- the sneakiest bastard in town.
He was caught by G-men
Shooting his semen
Where the cops would slip and fall down.

There once was a gaucho named Bruno,
Who said, "About sex, well, I do know,
Sheep are just fine,
Chickens, divine,
But iguanas are Numero Uno."

There once was a gay young Parisian
Who screwed an appendix incision,
And the girl of his choice
Could hardly rejoice
At the horrible lack of precision.

There once was a girl from Cornell
Whose teats were shaped like a bell.
When you touched them they shrunk,
Except when she was drunk,
And then they got bigger than hell.

There once was a girl from Decatur,
Who got laid by a big alligator.
Now nobody knew
The result of that screw,
'Cause after he laid her, he ate her.

There once was a girl from Madras
Who had such a beautiful ass -
It was not round and pink
(as you bastards think)
But had two ears, a tail, and ate grass.

There once was a girl from Spokane,
Went to bed with a one-legged man.
She said, "I know you—
You've really got two!
Why didn't you say so when we began?"

There once was a girl named Irene
Who lived on distilled kerosene
But she started absorbin'
A new hydrocarbon
And since then has never benzene.

There once was a girl named Louise
Whose pubics hung down to her knees
The crabs in her twat
Tied the hairs in a knot
And constructed a flying trapeze

There once was a girl named Mcgoffin
Who was diddled amazingly often.
She was rogered by scores
Who'd been turned down by whores,
And was finally screwed down in a coffin.

There once was a girl named Priscilla
Whose vagina was flavored vanilla.
The taste was so fine
Man and beast stood in line
(Including a stud armadilla).

There once was a girl so lovely,
Who wanted to make love in the bubbly,
She strapped on her tanks,
And started her pranks,
But the lobsters all thought she was ugly.

There once was a golfer named Leer,
Who was put in the clink for a year,
For an action obscene,
On the very first green.
Where the sign said "Enter course here."

There once was a gouty old colonel
Who grew glum when the weather grew vernal,
And he cried in his tiffin
That his prick wouldn't stiffen,
And the size of the thing was infernal.

There once was a guardsman from Buckingham
Who said, "As for girls, I hate fucking 'em.
But when I meet boys,
God! how I enjoys
Just licking their peckers and sucking 'em."

There once was a handsome young seaman
Who with ladies was really a demon.
In peace or in war,
At sea or on shore,
He could certainly dish out the semen.

There once was a horse name of Lily
Whose dingus was really a dilly.
It was vaginoid duply,
And labial quadruply —
In fact, he was really a filly.

There once was an aesthetic young miss,
Who thought it the apex of bliss,
To Jack herself silly,
With the bud of a Lily,
Then go in to the garden to piss,

There once was a husky young Viking
Whose sexual prowess was striking.
Every time he got hot
He would scour the twat
Of some girl that might be to his liking.

There once was a jolly old bloke
Who picked up a girl for a poke.
He took down her pants,
Fucked her into a trance,
Then pissed into her shoe for a joke.

There once was a lady from Exeter,
So pretty that men craned their necks at her.
One was even so brave
As to take out and wave
The distinguishing mark of his sex at her.

There once was a lady from Kansas
Whose cunt was as big as Bonanzas.
It was nine inches deep
And the sides were quite steep —
It had whiskers like General Carranza's.

There once was a lady named Clair,
Who possessed a magnificent pair.
Or that's what I thought,
Till I saw one get caught,
On a thorn and begin losing some air.

There once was a lady named Myrtle
Who had an affair with a turtle.
She had crabs, so they say,
In a year and a day
Which proved that that turtle was fertile.

There once was a virgin from Dover,
Who was had in the woods by a drover,
When the going got hard,
He greased her with lard,
Which felt nice, so they started all over.

There once was a lawyer named Rex
With minuscule organs of sex.
Arraigned for exposure,
He maintained with composure,
"De minimis non curat lex."
(Ed. the law does not concern itself with small things.)

There once was a lifeguard named Lee
Who rescued a girl from the sea
She asked how to pay,
And he said "Try this way,
Go down for the third time on me."

There once was a maid from Mobile
Whose cunt was made of blue steel.
She only got thrills
From pneumatic drills
And an off-centered emery wheel.

There once was a man from Bombay
He would do it all night and all day
But he soon became sore
And would then loudly roar
When his wife sucked his balls in play.

There once was a man from Calcutta
Who used to beat off in the gutta
The heat of the sun
Affected his gun
And turned all his cream into butta!

There once was a man from South Lick,
Who always ate soup with his prick.
He said "When I eat
Either fish, foul or flesh,
I otherwise finish too quick."

There once was a man from Exameter
Who had a prodigious diameter
But it wasn't the size
That brought forth the cries
'Twas his rhythm, iambic pentameter.

There once was a man from Madras,
Whose balls were made out of brass.
When they clanged together,
They played "Stormy Weather",
And lightning shot out of his ass.

There once was a man from Nantee
Who buggered an ape in a tree.
The results were most horrid
All ass and no forehead
Three balls and a purple goatee.

There once was a man from Nantucket
Who kept all his cash in a bucket.
His daughter, named Nan,
Ran away with a man,
And as for the bucket, Nantucket.

The pair of them went to Manhasset,
(Nan and the man with the asset.)
Pa followed them there,
But they left in a tear,
And as for the asset, Manhasset.

Pa followed the pair to Pawtucket,
(Nan and the man with the bucket.)
Pa said to the man,
"You're welcome to Nan."
But as for the bucket, Pawtucket.

There once was a man from Nantucket
Whose dick was so long he could suck it.
He said with a grin
As he wiped off his chin,
"If my ear was a cunt, I could fuck it."

There once was a man from Racine,
Who invented a screwing machine.
Both concave and convex,
It could please either sex,
But, oh, what a bastard to clean!

There once was a man from Sandem
Who was making his girl on a tandem.
At the peak of the make
She jammed on the brake
And scattered his semen at random.

There once was a man named McGruder,
Who canoed with a girl in Bermuder.
But the girl thought it crude,
To be wooed in the nude,
So McGru took an oar and subduder.

There once was a man named Parridge
With peculiar views on marriage.
He sucked off his brother,
Fucked his own mother,
And gobbled his sister's 'coutarge'.

There once was a man with a hernia
Who said to his doctor, "Gol dern ya,
When you work on my middle
Be sure you don't fiddle
With things that do not concern ya."

There once was a member of Mensa
Who was a most excellent fencer.
The sword that he used
Was his — (line is refused,
And has now been removed by the censor).

There once was a miner named Dave,
Who kept a dead whore in his cave.
She was ugly as shit,
And missing one tit,
But think of the money he saves.

There once was a monk of Camyre
Who was seized with a carnal desire
And the primary cause
Was the abbess's drawers
Which were hung up to dry by the fire.

There once was a newspaper vendor,
A person of dubious gender.
He would charge one-and-two
For permission to view
His remarkable double pudenda.

There once was a plumber from Leigh
Who was plumbing his maid by the sea.
Said she, "Please stop plumbing,
I think someone's coming!"
Said he, "Yes, I know love, it's me."

There once was a pretty young Mrs.
Whose tearful but short story this is.
Her mind lost its grasp -
Now she thinks she's an asp
And just sits in the corner and hrs.

There once was a queen of Bulgaria
Whose bush had grown hairier and hairier,
Till a prince from Peru
Who came up for a screw
Had to hunt for her cunt with a terrier.

There once was a reverend at Kings
Whose mind 'twas on heavenly things.
But his heart was on fire
For a girl in the choir
Whose tits were like jelly on springs.

There once was a sad Maitre d'hotel
Who said, "They can all go to hell!
What they do to my wife —
Why it ruins my life;
And the worst is they do it so well."

There once was a sailor named Gasted,
A swell guy, as long as he lasted,
He could jerk himself off
In a basket, aloft,
Or a breeches-buoy swung from the masthead.

There once was a Scot named McAmeter
With a tool of prodigious diameter.
It was not the size
That cause such surprise;
'Twas his rhythm — iambic pentameter.

There once was a spaceman named Spock
Who had a huge Vulcanized cock.
A girl from Missouri
Whose name was Uhura
Just fainted away from the shock.

There once was a Swede in Minneapolis,
Discovered his sex life was hapless:
The more he would screw
The more he'd want to,
And he feared he would soon be quite sapless.

There once was a whore from Regina
Who had a stupendous vagina.
To save herself time,
She had six at a time,
And another one working behind her.

There once was a yokel of North Weald,
Engaged to look after a field,
But he lurked in the ditches
And diddled the bitches
Now his balls are hung from a shield.

There once was a young fellow named Blaine,
And he screwed some disgusting old Jane.
She was ugly and smelly,
With an awful pot-belly,
But... well, they were caught in the rain.

There once was a young girl from Natches
Who chanced to be born with two snatches
She often said, "Shit!
I'd give either tit
For a guy with equipment that matches."

There once was a young man from Boston
Who drove around town in an Austin,
There was room for his ass,
And a gallon of gas,
So he hung out his balls and he lost 'em.

There once was a young man from France
Who waited ten years for his chance;
He got it one ex bono,
From a girl who said "No, no!
But I'll exchange a fuck for romance!"

There once was a young man from Yuma
Who attempted sex with a puma
He gave up real quick
Minus nose, toes, and prick
In obvious pain and ill huma.

There once was a young man from Yuma,
Who told an elephant joke to a puma.
Now his dry bleached bones lie,
Under hot Asian skies,
'Cause the puma had no sense of huma.

There once was a young man named Clyde
Who fell in an outhouse, and died.
He had a twin brother
Who fell in another
And now they're interred side by side.

There once was a young man named Lancelot
Whom the townsfolk would look at askance a lot
For when he should pass
A desirable lass
The front of his pants would advance a lot.

There once was an old man from Esser,
Who's knowledge grew lesser and lesser.
It at last grew so small,
He knew nothing at all,
And now he's a College Professor.

There once were two brothers named Luntz
Who buggered each other at once.
When asked to account
For this intricate mount,
They said, "Ass-holes are tighter than cunts."

There once were two women from Birmingham.
And this is the story concerning 'em.
They lifted the frock
And fondled the cock
Of the bishop as he was confirming 'em.

There was a bluestocking in Florence
Wrote anti-sex pamphlets in torrents,
Till a Spanish grandee,
Got her off with his knee,
And she burned all her works with abhorrence.

There was a family named Doe,
An ideal family to know.
As father screwed mother,
She said, "You're heavier than brother."
And he said, "Yes, Sis told me so!"

There was a fat lady of China
Who'd a really enormous vagina,
And when she was dead
They painted it red,
And used it for docking a liner.

There was a fat man from Rangoon
Whose prick was much like a balloon.
He tried hard to ride her
And when finally inside her
She thought she was pregnant too soon.

There was a gay countess of Bray,
And you may think it odd when I say,
That in spite of high station,
Rank and education,
She always spelled cunt with a 'k'.

There was a gay dog from Ontario
Who fancied himself a Lothario.
At a wench's glance
He'd snatch off his pants
And make for her Mons Venerio.

There was a gay parson of Tooting
Whose roe he was frequently shooting,
Till he married a lass
With a face like my arse,
And a cunt you could put a top-boot in.

There was a girl from Aberystwyth
Who brought grain to the mill to get grist with.
The miller's son Jack
Laid her flat on her back
And united the organs they pissed with.

There was a lewd fellow named Duff
Who loved to dive deep in the muff.
With his head in a whirl
He said, "Spread it, Pearl;
I cunt get enough of the stuff!"

There was a pianist named Liszt
Who played with one hand while he pissed,
But as he grew older
His technique grew bolder,
And in concert jacked off with his fist.

There was a poor parson from Goring,
Who made a small hole in his flooring,
Fur-lined it all round,
Then laid on the ground,
And declared it was cheaper than whoring.

There was a strong man of Drumrig
Who one day did seven times frig.
He buggered three sailors,
Four dogs and two tailors,
And ended by fucking a pig.

There was a teenager named Donna
Who never said, "No, I don't wanna."
Two days out of three
She would shoot LSD,
And on weekends she smoked marijuana.

There was a young belle of old Natchez
Whose garments were always in patchez.
When comment arose
On the state of her clothes
She, drawled, "When ah itchez, ah scratchez."

There was a young blade from South Greece
Whose bush did so greatly increase
That before he could shack
He must hunt needle in stack.
'Twas as bad as being obese.

There was a young bride, a Canuck,
Told her husband, "Let's do more than suck.
You say that I, maybe,
Can have my first baby—
Let's give up this Frenchin' and fuck!"

There was a young bride of Antigua
Whose husband said, "Dear me, how big you are!"
Said the girl, "What damn'd rot!
Why, you've only felt my twot,
My legs and my arse and my figua!"

There was a young chap in Arabia
Who courted a widow named Fabia.
"Yes, my tongue is as long
As the average man's dong,"
He said, licking the lips of her labia.

There was a young cook with the art
Of making a delicious tart
With a handful of shit,
Some snot and some spit,
And he'd flavor the whole with a fart.

There was a young damsel named Baker
Who was poked in a pew by a Quaker.
He yelled, "My God! what
Do you call this — a twat?
Why, the entrance is more than an acre!"

There was a young dolly named Molly
Who thought that to frig was a folly.
Said she, "Your pee-pee
Means nothing to me,
But I'll do it just to be jolly."

There was a young fellow from Cal.,
In bed with a passionate gal.
He leapt from the bed,
To the toilet he sped;
Said the gal, "What about me, old pal?"

There was a young fellow from Florida
Who liked a friend's wife, so he borrowed her.
When they got into bed
He cried, "God strike me dead!
This ain't a cunt — it's a corridor!"

There was a young fellow from Parma
Who was solemnly screwing his charmer.
Said the damsel demure,
"You'll excuse me, I'm sure,
But I must say you fuck like a farmer."

There was a young fellow name Tucker
Who, instructing a novice cock-sucker,
Said, "Don't bow out your lips
Like an elephant's hips,
The boys like it best when they pucker."

There was a young fellow named Ades
Whose favorite fruit was young maids.
But sheep, boys and whores,
And the knot holes in doors
Were by no means exempt from his raids.

There was a young fellow named Babbitt
Who could screw nine times like a rabbit,
But a girl from Johore
Could do it twice more,
Which was just enough extra to crab it.

There was a young fellow named Bliss
Whose sex life was strangely amiss,
For even with Venus His recalcitrant penis
Would never do better than t
h
i
s .

There was a young fellow named Bill,
Who took an atomic pill,
His navel corroded,
His asshole exploded,
And they found his nuts in Brazil.

There was a young fellow named Bowen
Whose pecker kept growin' and growin'.
It grew so tremendous,
So long and so pendulous,
'Twas no good for fuckin' — just showin'.

There was a young fellow named Brewer
Whose girl made her home in a sewer.
Thus he, the poor soul,
Could get into her hole,
And still not be able to screw her!

There was a young fellow named Case
Who entered a cunt-lapping race.
He licked his way clean
Through Number thirteen,
But then slipped and got pissed in the face.

There was a young fellow named Charteris
Put his hand where his young lady's garter is.
Said she, "I don't mind,
And higher up you'll find
The place where my fucker and farter is."

There was a young fellow named Cribbs
Whose cock was so big it had ribs.
They were inches apart,
And to suck it took art,
While to fuck it took forty-two trips.

There was a young fellow named dick
Who had a magnificent prick.
It was shaped like a prism
And shot so much gism
It made every cocksucker sick.

There was a young fellow named Feeney
Whose girl was a terrible meany.
The hatch of her snatch
Had a catch that would latch
- She could only be screwed by Houdini.

There was a young fellow named Fletcher,
Was reputed an infamous lecher.
When he'd take on a whore
She'd need a rebore,
And they'd carry him out on a stretcher.

There was a young fellow named Fyffe
Whose marriage was ruined for life,
For he had an aversion
To every perversion,
And only liked fucking his wife.

One year the poor woman struck,
She wept, and she cursed at her luck,
And said, "Where have you gotten us
With your goddamn monotonous
Fuck after fuck after fuck?

"I once knew a harlot named Lou —
And a versatile girl she was, too.
After ten years of whoredom
She perished of boredom
When she married a jackass like you!"

There was a young fellow named Gene
Who first picked his asshole quite clean.
He next picked his toes,
And lastly his nose,
And he never did wash in between.

There was a young fellow named Gluck
Who found himself shit out of luck.
Though he petted and wooed,
When he tried to get screwed
He found virgins just don't give a fuck.

There was a young fellow named Goody
Who claimed that he wouldn't, but would he?
If he found himself nude
With a gal in the mood
The question's not woody but could he?

There was a young fellow named Grant
Who was made like the sensitive plant.
When they asked "Do you fuck?"
He replied, "No such luck.
I would if I could, but I can't."

There was a young fellow named Grimes
Who fucked his girl seventeen times
In the course of a week —
And this isn't to speak
Of assorted venereal crimes.

There was a young fellow named Harry,
Had a joint that was long, huge and scary.
He grabbed him a virgin,
Who, without any urgin',
Immediately spread like a fairy.

There was a young fellow named Hatch
Who was fond of the music of Bach.
He said: "It's not fussy
Like Brahms and Debussy;
Sit down, and I'll play you a snatch."

There was a young fellow named Kimble
Whose prick was exceedingly nimble,
But fragile and slender,
And dainty and tender,
So he kept it encased in a thimble.

There was a young fellow named Meek
Who invented a lingual technique.
It drove women frantic,
And made them romantic,
And wore all the hair off his cheek.

There was a young fellow named Morgan
Who possessed an unusual organ:
The end of his dong,
Which was nine inches long,
Was tipped with the head of a gorgon.

There was a young fellow named Paul
Who confessed, "I have only one ball.
But the size of my prick
Is God's dirtiest trick,
For my girls always ask, 'Is that all?'"

Another young fellow named Paul,
Was able to bounce either ball,
He could stretch them and snap them,
And juggle and clap them,
Which earned him the plaudits of all.

There was a young lady at Court,
Who said to the King with a snort,
"Was it humour or shyness,
That prompted your highness,
To put Spanish Fly in my Port?"

There was a young lady of China,
Who mistook her mouth for her vagina,
Her clitoris huge,
She covered in rouge,
And lipsticked her labia minor.

There was a young fellow named Monk,
With a cock like and elephants trunk,
When it stiffened and rose,
It reached right up his nose,
And choked him with gallons of spunk

There was a young fellow named Pell
Who didn't like cunt very well.
He would finger or fuck one,
But never would suck one—
He just couldn't get used to the smell.

There was a young fellow named Price
Who dabbled in all sorts of vice.
He had virgins and boys
And mechanical toys,
And on Mondays... he meddled with mice!

There was a young fellow named Prynne
Whose prick was so short and so thin,
His wife found she needed
A Fuckoscope — she did —
To see if he'd gotten it in.

There was a young fellow of Harrow
Whose John was the size of a marrow.
He said to his tart,
"How's this for a start?
My balls are outside in a barrow."

other POWERFRESH titles

POWERFRESH TONI GOFFE TITLES

1902929411	FINISHED AT 50	2.99 ☐
1902929403	FARTING	2.99 ☐
190292942X	LIFE AFTER BABY	2.99 ☐

POWERFRESH MAD SERIES

1874125783	MAD TO BE FATHER	2.99 ☐
1874125694	MAD TO BE A MOTHER	2.99 ☐
1874126686	MAD ON FOOTBALL	2.99 ☐
187412552X	MAD TO GET MARRIED	2.99 ☐
1874125546	MAD TO HAVE A BABY	2.99 ☐
1874125619	MAD TO HAVE A PONY	2.99 ☐
1874125627	MAD TO HAVE A CAT	2.99 ☐
1874125643	MAD TO BE 40 HIM	2.99 ☐
1874125651	MAD TO BE 40 HER	2.99 ☐
187412566X	MAD TO BE 50 HIM	2.99 ☐

POWERFRESH FUNNYSIDE SERIES

1874125260	FUNNY SIDE OF 30	2.99 ☐
1874125104	FUNNY SIDE OF 40 HIM	2.99 ☐
1874125112	FUNNY SIDE OF 40 HER	2.99 ☐
190292911X	FUNNY SIDE OF 50 HIM	2.99 ☐
1874125139	FUNNY SIDE OF 50 HER	2.99 ☐
1874125252	FUNNY SIDE OF 60	2.99 ☐
1874125279	FUNNY SIDE OF SEX	2.99 ☐

POWERFRESH OTHER A5

1874125171	"CRINKLED "N" WRINKLED"	2.99 ☐
1874125376	A MOTHER NO FUN	2.99 ☐
1874125449	WE'RE GETTING MARRIED	2.99 ☐
1874125481	CAT CRAZY	2.99 ☐
190292908X	EVERYTHING MEN KNOW ABOUT SEX	2.99 ☐
1902929071	EVERYTHING MEN KNOW ABOUT WMN	2.99 ☐
1902929004	KISSING COURSE	2.99 ☐
1874125996	CONGRATULATIONS YOU'VE PASSED	2.99 ☐
1902929276	TOILET VISITORS BOOK	2.99 ☐
1902929160	BIG FAT SLEEPY CAT	2.99 ☐

POWERFRESH SILVEY JEX TITLES

1902929055	FART ATTACK	2.99 ☐
1874125961	LOVE & PASSION 4 THE ELDERLY	2.99 ☐
187412597X	A BABY BOOK	2.99 ☐
1874125996	SHEEP 'N' NASTY	2.99 ☐
1874125988	SPORT FOR THE ELDERLY	2.99 ☐
1902929144	FUN & FROLICS FOR THE ELDERLY	2.99 ☐
1902929756	IT'S A FUNNY OLD WORLD	3.99 ☐
1904967108	WRINKLIES RULE OK!	3.99 ☐

POWERFRESH HUMOUR

1874125945	GUIDE TO SEX & SEDUCTION	3.99 ☐
1874125848	DICK'S NAUGHTY BOOK	3.99 ☐
190292925X	MODERN BABES LB OF SPELLS	4.99 ☐
1902929268	A MUMS LB OF SPELLS	4.99 ☐
1904967000	NOT THE OXFORD DICTIONARY	4.99 ☐
1904967019	PESSIMISIMO	4.99 ☐

1904967027	POLITICAL BOLLOCKS	4.9
190496706X	POLITICALLY INCORRECT NOTICEBRD	3.9
1904967124	JIM CRAIG ON GOLF	3.9
1904967132	JIM CRAIG ON COFFEE	3.9

POWERFRESH LITTLE SQUARE TITLES

1902929330	LS DIRTY JOKES	2.5
1902929314	LS DRINKING JOKES	2.5
1902929322	LS GOLF JOKES	2.5
190292939X	LS IRISH JOKES	2.5
1902929292	LS TURNING 18	2.5
1902929977	LS TURNING 21	2.5
1902929969	LS THE BIG 30	2.5
1902929241	LS THE BIG 40	2.5
1902929233	LS THE BIG 50	2.5
1902929284	LS THE BIG 60	2.5
190292973X	LS DO YOU COME HERE OFTEN	2.5
1902929217	LS YES BUT...!	2.5
1902929306	LS WHISKY	2.5
1902929500	LS HOW TO PULL BY MAGIC	2.5
1904967051	LS PUB GAMES	2.5
1902929748	LS SEX SLANG	2.5

POWERFRESH STATIONARY TITLES

1902929381	WEDDING GUEST BOOK	9.9
1904967094	WEDDING PLANNER	9.9
1902929349	WEEKLY PLANNER CATS	6.9
1902929357	WEEKLY PLANNER DOGS	6.9
1902929365	WEEKLY PLANNER COTTAGES	6.9
1902929373	WEEKLY PLANNER OFFICE	6.9
1902929519	HUMDINGER TELEPHONE BOOK	4.9
1902929527	HUMDINGER ADDRESS BOOK	4.9
1902929535	HUMDINGER NOTEBOOK	2.9
1902929810	MODERN BABES ADDRESS BOOK	4.9
1902929802	MODERN BABES TELEPHONE BOOK	4.9
1902929829	MODERN BABES BIRTHDAY BOOK	4.9
1904967043	GARDENERS YEAR BOOK	4.9

Name

Address

P&P £1.00 Per Parcel
Please send cheques payable to Powerfresh LTD
To Powerfresh LTD Unit 3 Everdon Park,
Heartlands Industrial Estate, Daventry NN11 8YJ